Of the house

wisconsin poetry series

Edited by Ronald Wallace and Sean Bishop

molly spencer

If the house

THE UNIVERSITY OF WISCONSIN PRESS

The University of Wisconsin Press
728 State Street, Suite 443
Madison, Wisconsin 53706-1428
uwpress.wisc.edu

Gray's Inn House, 127 Clerkenwell Road
London EC1R 5DB, United Kingdom
eurospanbookstore.com

Printed in the United States of America
This book may be available in a digital edition.

Library of Congress Cataloging-in-Publication Data
Names: Spencer, Molly, author.
Title: If the house / Molly Spencer.
Other titles: Wisconsin poetry series.
Description: Madison, Wisconsin : The University of Wisconsin Press, [2019] | Series:
          Wisconsin poetry series
Identifiers: LCCN 2019011085 | ISBN 9780299325947 (pbk. : alk. paper)
Subjects: | LCGFT: Poetry.
Classification: LCC PS3619.P4658 A6 2019 | DDC 811/.6—dc23
LC record available at https://lccn.loc.gov/2019011085

this book is for my teachers

Deb Dieckman, who gave me a copy of Anne Sexton's
Selected Poems in high school

Valerie Sayers, who gave me an inkling

Tom Ruud, who called me poet

Deborah Keenan, who gave me process

Rick Barot, who gave me ambition

and David Biespiel, who gave me permission.
And courage.

> . . . & the roads kept thawing between snows
> In the first spring sun, & it was all, like spring,
> Irrevocable . . .

—Larry Levis

contents

I.

If I tell you everything, maybe as day fades,   3
Conversation with Lace Thong and Car Keys   4
Conversation with Glass and Joist   5
Silences: snowfall   6
Grisaille | August   8
Because I want to give them more than the small, gray stone   9
Moving Day   11
Love at These Coordinates   12
Disclosures | If you are aware of any settling   13

II.

Interior with a Woman Peeling Oranges, Snapping Beans   17
There Is Only One Word for Snow, but I Want More   23
Tentative Theories   24
Elegy with Edge Effects   25
Meditation at Fishtown   26
Meadow | A Reckoning   28

III.

Night Repairs   37
Conversation with Shower and Vestibule   38
Disclosures | If you are aware of any shared features   39
Disclosures | If you are aware of any nuisance animals such as
    crows, chickens, or barking dogs   40
Elegy Beginning with a Text from My Brother   42
As if life can go on as it has   44
Even so, the first bird   45

Elegy at the Strandline   47
Nocturne   48
Conversation with Distance and Shaking   49

IV.

Litany   53
Bridging   54
Meditation at Ice-Out   58

V.

Love Story   61
Disclosures | If the house is built on a hillside   63
In Southeast Lower Michigan, a Chance of Snow after Midnight 64
Vestige   65
Aubade   67
Address to the Meadow in the Dusk   68
Frank Next Door   69
Translation   71
Conversation with Windows and Green   72
How to Love the New House   74
I Talk Myself through the Facts of Each Day   75

Notes   77
Acknowledgments   81

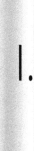

I.

If I tell you everything, maybe as day fades,

say dusk. If I say
ditch-weed, outskirts, field of

sting and bloom. How clouds pile on the ridge, sky
of a hundred grays, hill

of the watching and waiting.
Instructions for fire. If I tell you a leaf

in the table is a distance,
a prayer, milk and *all thy mercies.*

Tell you later, bedtime, corner
of the hall, saint in the corner, corner if a girl can dream

of sand and shoreline, drop-off, O indigo
blade. *Make us mindful*—that's how it goes. If I wait

for a storm, watch it blow over or watch it fall
open, the tumbling wind, the sky cracking. Don't cry,

little one, the milk-spill
is harmless, bridal

wash over dark wood,
moonlight shoaling

slow, pledged to the crack
where the leaf drops in, loose

devotion. Destined. Undaunted.
Then the slipping through.

Conversation with Lace Thong
and Car Keys

She is in the kitchen bent over
In a blue lace thong when he comes
Through the door blows by her forgot my keys he says

She says oh
She is standing up now having found
What she was looking for she forgets now what it was

Down the hall the *thunk* of a drawer
Opening the broken music of his hands
Running over its contents did you find them

She says yes he says good she says

Blows back through the kitchen
The keys jangle their little found song gotta go
He says bye she says bye

To a door already latched shut she says
To the ringing quiet I guess I'll get dressed now

It was seam tape she needed no it was
A pair of shears she slides into her jeans then she

Snips the loose thread at the crotch

Conversation with Glass and Joist

From her side of the bed she says tell me
This is years ago now he says what

Do you mean she says
Tell me something

What
Anything

Then the palpable glass
Of his silence and her words falling

From it like stunned birds then the sinking
Of another broken dusk down into night

By now the towers have fallen
There is a baby

In the next room nuzzling sleep
And her body

Has learned the meaning of both
Collapse and endure by now

She is accustomed to being the last
One up in a house

That settles and shifts
In the night the sigh and snap

Of a joist slackening
From its nail she says

To the glass to the falling
Night did you hear that

Silences: snowfall

It wasn't true—what did she always say—
that he was very dutiful.

She was the one who trapped the mice when they came inside, Novembers,
who shored up the fence where it sagged

like a lapsed vow
of edges. Those first winters

she showed him how to stoke a fire
in her body, but he must not have believed her.

He would always get dressed after
in deference to the no one else in the room.

Silences: snowfall, clock-stop, steam
on the windows.

She didn't even go out to watch him leave
seeds for the birds atop the new snow. And love

took its leave of her slowly,
as a tree lets drop its leaves in the autumn

of no wind. As a woman undresses
alone again, smooths her clothes on the end of the bed,

who has become practiced at remaining
still, as if being painted. Or carved.

This is how she learned the truth
of skin. Not its thinness

but its animal thirst—
the last time

he touched her
and she felt touched.

Grisaille | August

And if I ever make it back to low ground,
let it be that my body was tenderly
drawn there. Let it be because time held
itself in its hands. And the torn edge of the lake
stayed torn, the gull-cry, and the storm held off.

And if you find me there again sifting through
the worn consolations of driftwood
and strandline, if you think you hear me
singing and faintly singing, it will be a song
of what has lasted, of washed-over-and-still-here,

of stone, stone, and again, stone.

Because I want to give them more than the small, gray stone

of my sorrow, I take them to see the traveling exhibit,
the girl with the pearl on her ear.

I say, *Look*—the painted ground we thought was black is green.

Because there is fence I loved once, a fence
they no longer remember, I tell them: It was shadow-boxed, silvered,
worn soft by long years of storm.

In a dream of hands folding clothes
into a suitcase, there is always a stranger
adrift in the hall. In winter,

a dreamed-of house is almost as good
as a real one. Same with fire.

Because I know this, I give them a book
in which the way to save yourself is to choose
a different ending.

I leave them
to read it for themselves.

        O child
who sits on the landing
of my heart, the stairs are just another way
of saying, *Shall we go down?*

Of the girl we saw framed and hung
on the wall, I'm told she won't come this way again.

Of the fence, that it falls, is falling.

These are the stores I've gathered for you
like tight fists
of apples, globes of fat squash.

Given time they will ripen,
grow sweet, become something
for you to get by on.

Moving Day

Goodbye is the last box half-packed, is the front door left
open. Goodbye is this quiet procession of men packing
years of muted sun in the back of a truck again. Today
the light through the redwoods reminds you
of a gentle white pine you will never again climb.
Back then, when the sky seemed to pass over
like one long movie, weeks of uncomplicated blue,
then occasional warm rains. The crew boss calls you over,
shows you the loose leg of your grandfather's desk.
Yes, you say, it's been that way for years.
Which doesn't mean your heart won't lurch inside
the scuffed walls of you when he pulls the leg out
of its peg hole, shuts it in a drawer. More flaws
as the rooms take on a shabby cast. Now they are dismantling
the bed you've slept on for years. Their overheard grunts,
the shift and clang of parts coming loose. You've lived
this day before. Now is the time to look away
so you won't have to watch the broken body of it
lugged out into daylight once more—
headboard, footboard, wide golden flanks of its sides.

Love at These Coordinates

Put the window here. No

put it here. Where
the leaves are about to burn
and blow away. Keep sweeping

over the bare place
where
you thought you left

your body—breezeway
strike plate
tread of the stair.

Here is the sill
where at the end of

every winter I have tried
to force the paperwhites

to bloom.

Disclosures | If you are aware of any settling

After a while a wooded lot
means someday you will pay
to have the trees cut down.

The water spout on the door of the fridge
is just one more thing
that will break. These windows

are original, meaning
warped and in need
of repair.

Is there traffic noise, is there
airport noise, has the basement
ever flooded. Could the kids

bike to school. Why
is there all this unusable space
in the entry. You are tired

of trying to guess the reasons
they chose laminate
over hardwood

and the age of the furnace.
You would say
early two-thousands.

All the years it will take
for your hand to find the hall
light in the dark.

How the roof keeps
the rain off until it doesn't.
And winter nights—

the kids quiet in their beds,
the sliced blue threading
through inevitable cracks—

how you'll settle in front of the fire,
listening to its shift and fall,
staring into flames of your own making.

II.

Interior with a Woman Peeling Oranges, Snapping Beans

1.

They are not in season. Nothing is
in season. It's December. The oranges I couldn't resist
at the market, their extravagant glow, trucked in,
the green beans, trucked in

> [*extravagant*
> from the Latin for *outside of* + *to roam*].

I set the beans aside in the sink for rinsing, then
pull away the pliant skin
of one orange—

flesh broken,
bright and sweet.

2.

Out the kitchen window, winter has had the last word
with the songbirds and the gardens. Night begins
                    to drag over the sky.

While I complain about the city not plowing
my street after a foot of snow
                        the glaciers calve,

the water rusts just north of here.
The rebels' stronghold fails.
Awful things keep happening

everywhere   but not to me.

3.

It is winter there, too. I have seen the photos
of the little girl in her fuchsia coat,
                    whose color reminds me of the bougainvillea
that grew outside my last kitchen window, spilled bloom

against the plainsong snow.

I think her mother's bones must heave in their sockets—a pendulum
slowing—one way   then the other, toward
                    the curve of a tiny apricot cheek, then
toward the open mouth

of the mute   and patient earth.

4.

A city unroofed, ungardened.
        Unbodied. A city becomes a ruin

of a ruin of a city—dust of brick and dust
of bone, ash
of skin, sift
        of last page turning.

And people send their epitaphs
skyward, prophetic
        bits and bytes pinging down
through the star charts, blinking

on a small screen I've set nearby on the counter.
I pick it up to call the city about the snowed-in street and—

        help us
        they are dancing on our bodies

5.

It is not enough to want
to be good. Not enough to wish
I deserved the pitch of a roof overhead, a quiet

street. Tonight the whole world stands by and I stand by
the sink, snapping off the tapered ends of beans I'll feed to my children,
                                        six-thirty sharp,

then snapping them in half—tell me, how can I not
think of finger bones—
                        and in half again.

6.

Like small suns, the oranges flare
in their bowl on the counter.

It is easy enough to salt the beans
with my unearned tears.

Easy enough to remember holding
each orange in my hand at the market, saying,

These are as big as a baby's head!
Putting them in a plastic bag,

only five-for-a-dollar.

There Is Only One Word for Snow, but I Want More

If I could just describe the blunt edge
of a storm as it scrapes over land,
maybe I could stop watching

its approach from the crest
of a hill
I'm sure I've mentioned before.

In the moment the snow changes everything,
I want to feel again
the inmost woods—

when the black-boned trees are clothed in white again,
when the meadow blurs and kneels down.

When every roof becomes again a bride
to a sharp season.

The children have grown taller.
What was stone in me is ground to sand. This is why

I want winter to be holy and precise.
Even the longest winter—

crown on the ruins
                         of blossoms,

          altar cloth   penance   scalpel   caul

Tentative Theories

That the bridge will hold.

The river sliding past under ice—that months from now
the muscled arm of it will unclench
into ocean, having tried to carry
the thick earth all the way down.
Having mostly failed.

There are more varieties of ash than thorns
in a bramble. Think of all the things that will burn—
a hillside, dinner again, even the skin

in persistent wind. When the orchard unfolds
in a dream of blossoms, this means snow
has blown over the road in a storm. This means yes,

the color has drained from the sky
and a father's face.
All the smooth, untouched waters

of our lives are still ours.
And were never ours.

Sometimes a stone is only a stone.

Hold still, will you,
while I consult the map again.

That all the sundered boats remember open water and the wound
speaks of its own healing,

of put yourself back together. Now rise up
tender and gleam.

Elegy with Edge Effects

The sky is stone and the rain and, yes, I am blown here.

Stand of birch strung alongside the meadow, sodden,
not knowing what to do   with their hands

in this weather. I am here only to ask: What, edge
of the woods, did you ever mean to me?

There was something about cool silk. Sand
on a bare heel.   There was

something about the threshed
light through branches

when the rain stopped and the sun
            slid through, about more than one world

in the world. I keep trying to tell
                        about this and the call

of the bird more often seen than heard.

Meditation at Fishtown

Leland, Michigan

If I said blue.

If I said scuffed slate
cut across by blade after blade of rough sunlight.

If the wind were relentless. If a father stood amid

a thicket of docks clutching shore,
all the gray bones

of planking, and a girl stood with him,
watching the constellar shine of lines unspooling
as the town kids fish from the pier.

If a hook
from a failed cast catches his lip,

then a low *Hold on!* from his throat, flash
of one hand to grab the line, glint
of his quick knife to cut it.

If the barb sinks deep.

If the rose-trail of blood
down his chin is another river

you can't forget, you may never know

if the thick, green smell of depths here means *birth*
or *come-what-may*.

If the boats come in laden—
whitefish, lake trout, some still flicking their tails.

If a father has cut himself free.

If the boats here are named—hand-painted, block letters—
named GLORIA, named JOY.

Meadow | A Reckoning

Light sweep of breeze across one afternoon
Returns me. Come, meadow, rise and unfold,
Linen down the hill. Sing me your ditch songs—
Unspool, unspool. Shade of one oak edgewise,
Left standing, a watchtower for one scuff
On the curved earth. Once there was a girl here,
Thorned-over, sedge-sung, sunk in the tangle.
The small ongoing fact of her body
Just one of them—cricket, thistle, chicory,
Crow. Burr-hearted. All blooming and all fallow.
Hill and everything after. She is still
As one who knows she's native here.
Quiet as one who knows she's prey.

If a meadow, then a white house adrift
On the sea of one hill and a mother,
Strung sheets on the line. If a meadow, then
A back door unlatched, a way of seeing
Without being seen. Comings and goings
Of brothers and birds. Grind of tires, harsh
On gravel—a father, could be. Could be
A thief. One thing sure, the sun will fold up
Its cloth of light come evening. You can see
Until you can't anymore, then it's time
To go home. Then it's time to imagine
Or try to remember: there was a table
And a stubborn prayer. There was a roof that held
The night back. A cradle. Foot on the stair.

And the shore was an edge felt in the body.
The water's low, obsessive song, stone-strung.
Say *lapis*. Say *stung* with the windward chill
Of a long winter. Austere lace of waves
Windy days, capsized. Spill of the dune, trick
Of sun, a shadow backhanded on sand.
Gull and a gull and a flung gull above.
Tell me how to keep the breeze from meaning
Whole summers erased, to unravel the ruse
Of horizon. How the panic grass shakes
In wind. It's August again. You've become
A stark and slivered splay—tree the dune claimed
Year-wise, inch by inch, all the greening choked,
blown, gone. Yes, circled. Yes, starved then polished.

Somewhere in the meadow is everything
You believed in. Saints and worn stones. That cloth
Would hold and keep you warm come winter.
Roof that pinned in place the rooms of night. Milk,
Pale in a glass at table. Somewhere the spine
Of a girl uncurling, sprung scape in the sun.
There was a cage inside her for stung things—
Shinbone, door-slam, the picked-at scab of one
Heart letting drop its fixed number of beats
In red. There's no such thing as remembering
A meadow and walking it, too. It was
Only the scrap of one girlhood, worn sheet
Cut and tied in flags to keep the birds away
From a garden where winter broods in green.

Every last house with bone-bare walls. A fire
You left off tending. Another front door
Key lost in a storm. The slant of one night
Can silence a mother at her child's bed,
Can starve all the songs in the vault of her
Throat. She who remembers the aerial,
Pale seeds of milkweed, who has memorized
The thinness of skin. A winter marks time
Somewhere north of here. Somewhere a girl is
Perched on the landing, wrapping her small feet
In bread bags, pushing them into her boots.
There is a mother, sainted, somewhere
In a dream or down a hallway calling, *Try*.

You'll never convince the meadow of drop-off,
Though you've waded the shoals of her grasses
Recounting that cobalt blade, the slip down,
Milky shafts of surface light, profundal,
Your clenched heart ringing, a ship's bell, and all
The songs of sunken things in your held breath.
Those nights you'd wake, barely, in a back seat,
Blown waves of field after field washing by.
Somewhere a sky, somewhere a star falling.
Your father driving, loose rose of your mother,
Brothers drifting in downhill dreams. Gravel
Under slow tires. Your father's hands, most tender
Fact of him. Lifts you up and near, a skiff
Drifting, now beached on the shore of his heart.

Girl, you have burned yourself out. Goldenrod
Rusts at your edges, the dazed sky sharpens
Its blunted blade toward blue. Your father says,
A *forty-year roof*, meaning, *I will try*
To spare you this one trouble. Girl, the boat
Is tarped and stored for winter, oars stowed high
In the rafters. Yes, the sky will go down
To metal whole-cloth, each road anchor in
To its ground. For the faithless, there will be
Wind to believe in. For the haunted. There's
A place inside the body that can't forget,
A room where various pasts pick at the bones.
Girl, you won't feel a thing. The meadow will
Lie down. The first snows hardly ever stick.

Night Repairs

Little boat of the body,
anchor in,

the lake is stilling.

The night-birds call out
their bruised songs.
Even if they are not for you,

they will sound
against your wales,
fill your hollow.

Body, lower your weight
all the way down—
scraped keel

of you, nails clenched
to mend the holes
in your hull.

Don't ask
whether the lake's rolling swells
mean *to cradle* or *to lull.*

There's a road near here
called Deadstream

where the night runs
deeper for the leaf-shade.

I will make a note of this
two-laned sorrow

and how it spills away from the water.

Conversation with Shower and Vestibule

From his side of the bed he says how do you feel
About the shower she says what do you mean
He says I mean getting in it together conflicted she says

And that is the end
Of that while the rain

Falls no that's just the sprinkler he says are you asleep
She could answer but she is
Thinking about the last time

They moved together it was years ago now
How the heat bore down like a long dull labor and
The thick air clung wet to her skin and hair

Like regrets he says are you asleep again
She says nothing

Next morning checking realty sites
This one looks good he says

No why because I've had enough
Of patched screens and the little gasps

Of roofs at night she says I want a narrow
Empty place made for entering it's called a vestibule

She says and I will press my hands along its walls
In the dark if I have to

You are not being helpful he says I am
Being honest she says I am looking for a room
To walk away through see this

Tool in my hand see these nails I am driving them in hard
Under my feet as I go

Disclosures | If you are aware of any shared features

A driveway, for example, or a garden
wall. A fence, a heritage tree in the easement

of the heart, or a landscape convening
in the window, sunset on the blue foothills. Look

at Orion slung low tonight.
Look at the moon's milked light.

Or a cradle, a child's shifts and sighs
in sleep. An alcove—is that us

in the photo, smiling
on the porch. If there is only one

side of the bed. When you walk the hall
to the bedroom, one darkness,

alchemical. Spill of stones
on the sill, their one erosional fate.

One set of hands to test
the child's brow in fever. One sink

at which to stand wiping plates. A single mouth to taste
the dust of those words again—*for poorer   till death.*

Or a breastbone—as if *to cleave*
did not mean *to make a way through by splitting*

apart. As if it did not also mean
stick fast to.

Disclosures | If you are aware of any nuisance animals such as crows, chickens, or barking dogs

The crows will go on gathering
inside you. The crows will repeat
and repeat their hooked songs—

> *when in the interior*
> *who amidst the birches*
> *why   why   deadfall   why*

The crows will creak and rasp
like hinges. You'll wake to
days that stain your hands, bits of char

from a beach-fire, some forgotten summer. Days
that, like the crows, want answers—

> *if in the understory*
> *where the front crosses over the sky above you*
> *if you have untied your heart from the blood-knot*
> *and left the strings loose*
> *and desultory   now what*

The crows will follow you home wanting to know

> *are you happy now are you   happy*

Now that you've lost your faith in the slope
of the roof. Now that it's snowing
again and the whole world pretends

to soften. The crows will preside over your quiet
ritual of diminishment, calling out
sharp threats—

> *if by rafter   you mean rib*

If the moan of a northing train
is what's left to listen to. If it's a different train now
but just as forlorn.

Now that the only scrape of a shovel over the walk before daylight
is your scrape.

Now that the blade in your hands is the blade that you asked for.

Elegy Beginning with a Text from My Brother

how was the snow

As if the snow were a province I'd visited,
not a season come down upon me. As if
he'd never stood on the ridge and watched

the whole cloth of it blow in
over the lake,
blank and bridal.

Any mark I'd made on the earth, it annulled.
The dropped map, the poor footprints of children,
the felts I pulled from their boots hoping they'd dry

by morning. The snow was a field
I woke in. Here are the drifts
of my hands for proof, here is my heart gone

to windbreak. Brother, I am tired
of living bone-bound and uphill, of rolling through stops
to keep from getting stuck.

The snow was irrevocable, songless.

A relic. The ruins
of the wood.

I made my way home
by ditch and by deadfall,
all night laid awake in the storm

listening for the scrape
of the plow gone by, waiting
for the blade and my body

to change the snow's tense
from *falling and falling*
to *fell*.

As if life can go on as it has

The earth has all these endings.
The sparrows drop, the lilies lie down in a ditch.

In the daylight, a two-lane highway confirms all
its nouns: dregs of an orchard, barn dissolving, tract homes

conjured from forsaken fields. I am
in a kitchen's heavy afternoon

light. As if life can go on as it has, I sing. I stir
a pungent sauce the exact shade of love

or fear. The children pepper me with *whys*
and *hows*. The stove fan swallows what rises.

Even so, the first bird

In the west, etched and bony light of moonset.
East, warm breath of sun

                  fleshing the sky. Nothing

will ever be as legible
as these hills, still
black with their faith in themselves,

          even as the stars drift

away again. Even as children wash up
on beaches. All those gunned down.
Even the fires, the gaining seas,

the waters churning
between one heart
and the next
               heart, silt settling in the low spots—

Even so, the first bird has begun
the oldest song. A light

flicks on
over a sink.
Someone is awake

            somewhere. Today is Wednesday. My body

adds itself again to the unfolding
rooms of time,
foot on the stair. This is how to go on

breaking
with the broken world—

little spun
ball, lifeboat, faithful, fist
full of wildflowers with their roots pulled loose.

Elegy at the Strandline

I've kept from you the loose raft of my sorrow.
Kept the river, the fallen tree for crossing.

October and the birds flock
and rise, whole-cloth.

The birches revise themselves for winter.
Because your heart is anchored

in the harbor and you've never plied the trade winds
of my eyes, love can't make it rain

or not rain. Love can't make a road
end up at home.

Every day just shallow breaths
of light and all the gulls scavenging

the strandline, where
I have counted all the times

you didn't touch me. Where
I have stood on shore

years and seasons, windward.
Don't pretend this sand was never stone.

Nocturne

There is no absence that cannot be
replaced. The horizon fails

nightward. Later the moon,
faint, the faltering hull

of another day rowing
slowly away,

dirge in the rib. Where once
his mouth left its mark

on the tentative shore
of your body,

dusk-hues murmur
all the colors of a wound.

Conversation with Distance and Shaking

She rolls off him to her side of the bed that was good he says
She says did you close and lock the back door

His footsteps down the bleak hall
Of a night she knows by heart she thinks of distances

How they start with ordinary things silk
Over skin even a thin silk the inevitable shift

Of sand during storm done he says
And winters with your back to the shore how the ice is strong

Enough to hold you until it's not then you break
Through to another farther world are you awake he says

She says you have more time than you think
You have to swim yourself up out of the hole then roll

Away then crawl she says or if that fails
Get your arms up out of the water reach

As far as you can he says what are you talking about
So winter can hold you in place she says

So maybe someone will find you
You have about an hour he says why

Are you telling me this she says no one is dead
Until they're warm and dead he says jesus he rolls over

To his side of the bed she says next they will warm your body
Slowly this is called revival it means to live

Again she says then they'll shake you
Gently they'll say can you hear me

Can you hear me and if you can
You will have to admit that you can

IV.

Litany

What is your favorite word for *lost*. Corner, crow's call, lee of the hill.

What do you think the poet meant—*if the knot I tie is the wrong knot*. Was it winter then, too, did he speak from the unsteady raft of his sleep, do you.

Do you know the word for the bare winter days after leaf-fall but before the snows settle.

If the only rhyme were wrong-bodied, would you use it. Would you ink it black on the birch-white page. If the only word were *collide*.

Is it cold and nameless here tonight.

Is it like living in the space between ribs—*Where in the gust, the whirlwind, and the flaw.*

Have you dreamt it—the birches' twist and whip and how a gale roams through the dim townships breaking small branches.

Have you ever seen the snow as it drifts over mile roads sadden toward blue in the dusk-light. Cobalt tamed a bit with white. Have you tried to render it.

At the winter grave, with a stone in your hand, in the low glide of late sun aslant, have you placed stone on stone tasting the salt of my name. My name, whose meaning is *bitter*.

Did you think you could quiet the wind in me, your face in profile, your eyes on the distance. You whose name means *beloved*.

Bridging

Let it be early, before the birds begin,
and the night sky still
rashed with stars. Let the children sleep
while he packs the car for the drive back
to the house you've come to terms with, a day's drive
from here, a day and the edge of one night,
which is where you are now, standing
with your mother in the driveway while the men
carry the children—one, two, three dream-soft
bodies—settle them into their seats, tuck
them in snug under blankets. When they wake
you'll be hours from here, having crossed
a body of water deep enough to swallow
whole towns, wide enough to spawn legends
of mothers reaching shore without their children,
of children seen as islands from the shore.

2.

You've been trying to get this right—August
evening, ten o'clock and the sky
still rinsed with light. Inside the house,
the shadows have their way, ink brimming
into the contours of life, bone-black
shapes of table, lamp, eventual silhouette
of your father, backlit in the window as you sit
together remembering, in the hushed tones
dusk and the end of summer
seem to ask for, other Augusts far
from here, but not so far you can't
reel them back in if you each offer
scraps for the piecing—
it was the rowboat, wasn't it? It was
raining. No,
it's your daughter

3.

in the back seat saying, *Tell me a story.* When I was a girl
it was always summer. The sand
stayed warm past dark and the lake, too.
There was a small boat moored
to a large rock. There was a family there,
a picnic, a transistor radio
promising storm. There was a house on shore
they never went back to. The father
grew into tall pine, the mother made
of her body a sail. The brothers built a fire
of driftwood and sticks. The gulls
bickered, wanting the scraps. The girl
is still there hovering
over the scene, outcast, witness, wavering
angel—whether to be water,
whether to be bridge.

4.

Look back and everything stands
for something. The sable scrawl of trees
for the scar a stone left in your skin, curved
flank of the dune for the sand-strewn
bed you woke in then. The islands emerge
from the dark like children wandering
out of the room of their sleep into a kitchen, cusp
of morning. *Hog Island, Les Cheneaux*—
say their names and they begin
to mean something, edges shifting,
edges making themselves known. A sigh
from the back seat returns you
to the brink of day breaking—
cinder, stone, plum, shell, wound. The crest
of the bridge behind you now, and soon
the hunger begins in earnest.

Meditation at Ice-Out

Write a poem about the sounds the ice makes
end of winter, my father says.

If I said grinds like slow gears.

If I said moans and grieves, cracks
like a gun in the night but holds,
I would not be wrong.

There's a remedy for winter called the tilting of the earth.

It is not a sign of anything
and I don't blame the hills for cresting and falling
headlong through the seasons, nor the ditches

for revealing the dregs of our lives—
receipts for eggs and milk, a torn baseball, always just one shoe.

There's a story stowed in my mother's throat
about resurrection.
How we'll walk the earth again in clement light.

But spring unravels
the plot line. The trees look sickly. The roadkill,
which the snow had covered, gleams again like a used womb.

It's true I've chosen what's seen
over seeing. That's all my battered psalms are—stone
and lament.

In the end,
it's a quiet thing—the ice slipping loose
into water.

V.

Love Story

Now you are four in a boat.
Cut of heartwood.

Love bears down,
a slow storm.

This is in the time of no oars.
Past the point

of endless questions, one more story
            before bed. Only
chipped songs,
                    birds and complaints, lisp
of wave against gunwale. Love

                a low rolling
prayer of gray   and gray and gray.

This is in the time of finish your homework,
hang up your jacket, I said to fold the fucking socks.

Hook and line love—
give a boy a fish,
            teach a boy to catch fish.

                Love like a thinning
sheet, fitful, knotted
nights in the worn bed
of a life
                you can't take back.

In the time of becalming.
Which means *heat of the midday sun.*

Bootstrap love, cinder love, love

that knows everyone's heart
is the size and shape of a fist.

Disclosures | If the house is built on a hillside

You will have to make your peace with the tilt, the long fingers
earth draws over the skin.   And the rain—

      its drag and chant down the slope
of another night pooling   into blue-black.

All along your exteriors, the windows
will make their usual confessions—
      it was the birches. It was the wind. The fire

is meek, smokeless, kindled by a switch
on the wall, where you will feel compelled to sketch the snapped wings
      of your doubt. If it's prayer

you need, you will have to intone your own
makeshift *Nunc Dimittis*. Excise the *Domine*,
the *oculi*, *pace*, wrestle it, if you must, from the long swept hall

      of your throat. Then
tell the children the roof was built for this
weather.   Maybe they'll believe.

      That the clock
spools out the days then sets them back
to zero.   That hands are for holding

out in front of you in the unlit
hours like lamps. Or allegations. Little spells.
You will have to teach them how to thread

      tenderly down the stairwell's strict geometries
like light   through the charted rooms   of space.

      Show them how   to slip
out the back door soundlessly. Sidelong. Like a trespasser
                through a loose gate.

In Southeast Lower Michigan, a Chance of Snow after Midnight

The wind repeats itself
                  and repeats itself, galloping down
all the usual causeways. Those on the outskirts

remain vigilant on the outskirts, renewing their vows
to the outposts.
                Night will pass

by—a boat low in the water, motor cut—whether or not you sleep,
whether or not you sense the snow beginning, twinge
in the dream, twinge in the trapezium

bone of the left hand. When the day comes, it will break
               too bright—the light insisting
on perimeters, every branch and ledge handfasted

to itself in white and shriven, shriven.

                            Where the creek still sings
          its little broken song underneath,   just look
at what these winters have done

                to me. Here I am
standing on the snow where it has fallen
thick over the creek   and crusted.

Vestige

Let this be the only record left of us: The snows fell
into the nicked skin of the lake all day.

But the wind didn't throw us into tailspin. Like gulls, we knew
how to hang and kite in the air.

The way the snow fell, blurring the landscape, meant nothing. Its sibilance,
    nothing.
The way it kept falling and dissolving, falling and—

I have always known the horizon
is only a notional line.

There was no bridge lithe enough, nothing to span the burnished light I kept
seeing in a half-dream of you, sunlit. Your face in shadow, hands in shadow. Your
    eyes.

No skiff of light drifting in toward land where the longing
kept washing ashore, saying, *still, still, still.*

If I see you again, it will be for tonguing the word *cleave*
against your neck just behind the rosy lobe of your ear.

I won't know what to say about the daylight, the way it keeps arriving,
scraped and on its knees, through the skeletal trees.

It will be for tracing the languid paths
we drew on each other's skin as a means of committing a body to memory.

This bruise, you'll say,
Which rib?

Love, let me taste for the last time the weathered edges
of you under a low sky, a sky faltering

between *anchor* and *no longer*. Under a sky
sifting down its message in illegible scraps. Then let me turn

away, haltingly, let me go.
As the last boat before winter tacks into the wind this way, into the wind
    that way.

As a sail makes of headwind a crossing. Now
count all the years of your life that will bear no trace of me.

Aubade

In the end one cannot keep this love
concealed. Smoke unties

from ember, then
morning. You wake alone,

breeze and consolation, loose
in your white cotton. Light

gives the shape of *hill*
back to the hill. The quiet

skin remembers
and remembers—blue

of chicory flooding
its petals.

Address to the Meadow in the Dusk

I see what you're doing, growing thick with fire-
flies, trying to make me believe in some alternate night

sky. I've worn my heart's armor—stone
and thorn—against all your predictable disavowals,

your loose roots, petals weathered and falling
to dust in the bled vesper-light of evening,

faded sheet of you. I, too, want to shine a little
before dying, to sway in the uncountable

hands of the breeze. O clung-to diaspora of seeds,
prodigal, I have memorized the fitful angles

of your sand burr. I am resigned
to pulling you out of the cloth of me all winter

long, as an animal troubles a wound.
Where a two-track leaves the broad flank of you

behind, meadow, where you go down
to marry your one blue love,

that is where the world can bear
my weight. There I will lie down waiting

for the first dawn
with a blade in its wind.

Frank Next Door

After Dick Allen

The dishes are done, the counter wiped,
the children are all at school. The window is open
to a mild morning breeze, construction noise,
the many wars and storms that pound the earth.
But what I need to know, Frank next door,
is why have you torn out your lawn?
Also, am I my neighbor's keeper? And why
do we now say *three times* instead of *thrice*? As in,
thrice you have bent your eighty-nine years, your stooped back
over the same tired patch of grass between our houses.
Three times you have pulled it out by hand.
Frank, I'm up early, I know it's you
I hear at six a.m. with the *scritch-scritch*
of your rake and the occasional hollow *thunk*
of one of my boy's balls that you've thrown back over
to our side of the fence. Thank you, Frank,
but can I ask—why did you not stop with the grass? Why
have you tipped and unpotted all your leggy geraniums,
which I had come to admire for their infrequent orange blooms?
Was it you who came upon Ophelia sewing?
Fierce and uncertain, your shirt unbuttoned, hair raised
like a sail from sleep. Or madness. And Frank,
how is Barbara? It's been months since I've seen her
on your porch in her blue housedress. Do you know, Frank,
how hard it is to explain the concept of housedress
to today's kids? I confess, I believed myself up to the task—
I of sweep and mop, I of apron, of the homemade cupcakes
I brought to my daughter's class, about which a little girl asked,
Can't you afford *real* cupcakes? Of housedress I explained:
a simple garment, a row of buttons, often faded, never mind. But Frank,
about your camellia—that too? Despite its great red eyes
that open twice a year? Frank, the glossy leaves,
the smooth, layered buds before they flower.
How fastened they are, how pleasing in their closedness.

And what means this, my neighbor—
that you have left the bindweed climbing over our shared fence?
That squatter, that stowaway creeper has staked its claim
as "the worst weed in California." Frank, what I'm asking is,
are you shuffling off your mortal coil? Should I
start bringing casseroles? Is it so long a life? Did you know
it's also called creeping jenny, bellbine, sheepbine, and cornbind?
Don't you love such words? Frank next door,
is it wrong for me to find the bindweed oddly beautiful—
its scrawny persistence, all its trailing arms and legs,
the weak white faces of its blooms as they open to show
a curved swirl of blood at their throats?

Translation

When the house wakes hollow
with quiet, this is a name
spoken in the dark. The black
hills rolling toward blue means
another morning will drape
itself over the map. When the sun
soaks through lifting clouds,
when the sun falls to pieces
of gold on the floor, this is time
to wake the children
for the thousand natural shocks
that roam the earth.
No immediate threat to land
is a storm sharpening
over water. Cease-fire
means let us all go home
and sleep in our skittish beds
for one night. Compass
means learn what you can
from the word *north*.
Extraordinary circumstances
is a boy face down in the street,
a black boy, a four-hour pool of blood.
At the end of the road is recall
the last known coordinates
of the ones you love
or are supposed to love. Once
the word *dwell* meant *to lead
astray*. When the shaking starts, this is
let us make ourselves a home
here on the hillside.

Conversation with Windows and Green

Let's buy the Cape Cod in town he says she says
Let's buy the mid-century on the river bluff

It needs too much work he says
She says it understands distances depths he says

What are you talking about the windows
She says the way the light milks in

Thin through the trees and past them
The deep cut which is river

And the cladding around the fireplace
How the rough stones speak

Of the body she says also it's on the bus line
He shakes his head which is like saying

I will never understand you
She says remember last summer

When we took the kids down
To the river and you

Told them not to go in no he says
She says I do I let them go in

Anyway while you stood on the bank
Shaking your head and I went in too

She says I went in so they would know more
Than the shore so they would

Know the green insistent pull of river
Over skin why

Can't you just be happy he says she says
And also to keep them from drowning

How to Love the New House

Slantwise

Along the blade

Made of moonlight

With open eyes

By groping along

Only at night

Until your whole body knows it

Without a sound

On the table, the floor

With your ear to the door

When everyone's sleeping

Propped open

With both hands

In the arched darkness

On the stairwell

On your hands and knees

Until you ache with it

For the life of you

Until it shines

I Talk Myself through the Facts of Each Day

Here is a peach
fat in my hand. This means
it must be August.

Here is a child, new fruit
and soft, calling me *Mama*,
climbing up into my lap.

I can't see the singing
blackbird, but I hear
its tin song

so I believe
it is near, the way I believe in the pier—that it will hold
despite the water's prodigious gray

lull and pull—and the way I believe
a single word can rescue.

A word like *spandrel*.

A word like *thigh*.

This table
where I sit all through the slant

amber afternoon—it is a table
I chose
again this morning.

When you said, *Sleep*,
I almost believed
I could. *Be still.*

> [Here, say something
>   about a peach   over-softening, or a child
>
>   lengthening, or the verb *to climb*,
>   which means *to go up*   *by clinging*]

The facts of each day come to rest
all around me, fallen,
rust petals of the ditch, lily.

notes

The epigraph for the collection is from Larry Levis's poem "Gossip in the Village," from his posthumous collection *The Darkening Trapeze: Last Poems* (Saint Paul, MN: Graywolf Press, 2016).

Etymological references throughout the collection are from *The Barnhart Concise Dictionary of Etymology*, edited by Robert K. Barnhart (New York: HarperCollins, 1995) and/or etymonline.com.

"If I tell you everything, maybe as day fades,": This poem is indebted to Stanley Plumly's poem "Say Summer / For My Mother," from his collection *Out-of-the-Body Travel* (New York: The Ecco Press, 1977). The phrases "Make us mindful" and "all thy mercies" are from the Episcopal "Grace Before Meals" in the *Book of Common Prayer*.

"Disclosures": The subtitles for each of these poems are from the State of California seller's disclosures documents required for real estate transactions.

"Grisaille | August": Grisaille is a method of painting in gray monochrome.

"Because I want to give them more than the small, gray stone": The question, "Shall we go down?" is Tom Ruud's, from his poem "A Gnostic Gospel" in *Unable for the World to Sleep* (St. Paul, MN: The Laurel Poetry Collective, 2005).

"Interior with a Woman Peeling Oranges, Snapping Beans": In section four, the lines "help us / they are dancing on our bodies" are taken from NPR's live coverage of the fall of Aleppo in December of 2016, during which the anchors read aloud Tweets coming out of Aleppo as the city, which had been held by rebel forces, fell into the hands of the Assad regime. These lines are from two of those Tweets.

"Elegy with Edge Effects": Edge effects are changes in ecological populations and/or community structures that occur at the boundary of two habitats.

"As if life can go on as it has": The opening line of this poem is patterned off of the opening line of section nine of Rick Barot's poem "Like a Fire That Consumes All Before It," from his collection *Want* (Louisville, KY: Sarabande Books, 2008). Barot's line is, "The sky has all these beginnings."

"Nocturne": The phrase "There is no absence that cannot be replaced" is from René Char's poem "Chain," from *Selected Poems*, translated by Mary Ann Caws and Tina Jolas (New York: New Directions, 1992).

"Conversation with Distance and Shaking": This poem is indebted to an article from the *New York Times Magazine*, "How to Survive Falling through the Ice," by Malia Wollan, February 12, 2016.

"Litany": The text "if the knot I tie is the wrong knot" is from Charles Wright's poem "Hawaii Dantesca," from his collection *The Southern Cross* (New York: Random House, 1981). The text "Where in the gust, the whirlwind, and the flaw" is from John Keats' poem "On a Dream." The word for the bare winter days after leaf-fall but before snow falls is *barvinterdagar*, a Swedish word I learned of reading Robert Hass's essay "Tranströmer's *Baltics*: Making a Form of Time," from *Poets Teaching Poets: Self and the World*, edited by Gregory Orr and Ellen Bryant Voight (Ann Arbor: University of Michigan Press, 1996).

"Bridging": The legend referred to in section one is an Ojibwe legend about the formation of the Sleeping Bear Dunes and the Manitou Islands in northwest lower Michigan's Leelanau County. In section four, the Les Cheneaux Islands are in the Straits of Mackinac off the southernmost coast of Michigan's upper peninsula, near Cedarville; Hog Island is in Lake Michigan, due west of Mackinaw City, in Charlevoix County.

"Disclosures | If the house is built on a hillside": The *Nunc Dimittis*, also known as the Canticle of Simeon, is a prayer from the Roman Catholic Liturgy of the Hours, taken from the Gospel of Luke and traditionally recited at Compline (Night Prayer). The phrase *Nunc Dimittis* comes from the Latin Vulgate, "Nunc dimittis servum tuum, Domine," which is commonly translated, "Now, Lord, you let your servant go in peace." The Latin words *Domine*, *oculi*, and *pace* translate to "Lord," "eyes," and "peace," respectively.

"In Southeast Lower Michigan, a Chance of Snow after Midnight": The phrase "just look at what these winters have done to me" is patterned off a phrase from Vievee Francis's poem "Everywhere and Here Too," *Blueshift Journal* 6 (Winter 2017). Her phrase is "Just look what the mountains have done to me."

"Aubade": The phrase "In the end one cannot keep this love concealed" is from Zbigniew Herbert's poem "Stool," from his *Selected Poems*, translated by Czesław Miłosz and Peter Dale Scott (New York: Ecco Press, 1968).

"Address to the Meadow in the Dusk": The opening of this poem is indebted to Kelly Cressio-Moeller's poem "Letter to Low Tide," which the poet kindly shared with me in draft form and which appeared in *Cider Press Review* 19, no. 3 (October 2017).

"Frank Next Door": This poem is after Dick Allen's poem "Amy at the Front Desk," which I read in *Gettysburg Review* 27, no. 3 (Autumn 2014). This poem also borrows several phrases and grammatical constructions from Shakespeare's *Hamlet*.

"Translation": The phrase "thousand natural shocks" is from Shakespeare's *Hamlet*.

"How to Love the New House": This poem borrows formal elements from Billie Swift's poem "How to Take Pity," which the poet kindly shared with me in draft form and which appears in her chapbook *Everything Here* (Little Rock, AR: Sibling Rivalry Press, 2019).

acknowledgments

My thanks to the editors and staff at the following journals where these poems first appeared:

Cave Wall: "In Southeast Lower Michigan, a Chance of Snow after Midnight"

Copper Nickel: "Disclosures | If you are aware of any nuisance animals such as crows, chickens, or barking dogs"

FIELD: "Conversation with Shower and Vestibule"; "Conversation with Distance and Shaking"; "Conversation with Windows and Green"

The Georgia Review: "Address to the Meadow in the Dusk"; "Elegy Beginning with a Text from My Brother"; "[Somewhere in the meadow is everything]," from "Meadow | A Reckoning"

Gettysburg Review: "Disclosures | If you are aware of any shared features"; "Disclosures | If the house is built on a hillside"

On the Seawall: "Bridging"

Pleiades: "Meditation at Fishtown"

Ploughshares: "Meditation at Ice-Out"

Poetry Northwest: "Night Repairs"; "Tentative Theories"

Prairie Schooner: "Conversation with Lace Thong and Car Keys"; "Conversation with Glass and Joist"; "Elegy at the Strandline"; "I Talk Myself through the Facts of Each Day"; "Love Story"

Rise Up Review: "Even so, the first bird"

ZYZZYVA: "As if life can go on as it has"; "Frank Next Door"; "Disclosures | If you are aware of any settling"

"Interior with a Woman Peeling Oranges, Snapping Beans" won the 2018 Poetry Society of America Lucile Medwick Memorial Award, judged by Maggie Smith.

"Elegy Beginning with a Text from My Brother" also appreared at Poetry Daily.

"Tentative Theories" also appeared at *Vandal Poetry*.

"Frank Next Door" is for Ellen Bass.

Thank you to everyone at the Rainier Writing Workshop, especially Rick Barot for your belief in my work, and David Biespiel for keeping me out of my own way. Thank you to Vermont Studio Center for time and space to write. Thank you to Ron Wallace, Sean Bishop, and Dennis Lloyd, and everyone at University of Wisconsin Press for bringing this book into the world with such care. And deep gratitude to Carl Phillips, whose sentences and syntax I've been studying for years—thank you for reading these poems and saying yes to them.

wisconsin poetry series

Edited by Ronald Wallace and Sean Bishop

How the End First Showed (B) • D. M. Aderibigbe

New Jersey (B) • Betsy Andrews

Salt (B) • Renée Ashley

Horizon Note (B) • Robin Behn

About Crows (FP) • Craig Blais

Mrs. Dumpty (FP) • Chana Bloch

The Declarable Future (4L) • Jennifer Boyden

The Mouths of Grazing Things (B) • Jennifer Boyden

Help Is on the Way (4L) • John Brehm

Sea of Faith (B) • John Brehm

Reunion (FP) • Fleda Brown

Brief Landing on the Earth's Surface (B) • Juanita Brunk

Ejo: Poems, Rwanda, 1991–1994 (FP) • Derick Burleson

Jagged with Love (B) • Susanna Childress

Almost Nothing to Be Scared Of (4L) • David Clewell

The Low End of Higher Things • David Clewell

Now We're Getting Somewhere (FP) • David Clewell

Taken Somehow by Surprise (4L) • David Clewell

Borrowed Dress (FP) • Cathy Colman

Dear Terror, Dear Splendor • Melissa Crowe

Places/Everyone (B) • Jim Daniels

Show and Tell • Jim Daniels

Darkroom (B) • Jazzy Danziger

And Her Soul Out of Nothing (B) • Olena Kalytiak Davis

My Favorite Tyrants (B) • Joanne Diaz

(B) = Winner of the Brittingham Prize in Poetry
(FP) = Winner of the Felix Pollak Prize in Poetry
(4L) = Winner of the Four Lakes Prize in Poetry

Talking to Strangers (B) • Patricia Dobler

The Golden Coin (4L) • Alan Feldman

Immortality (4L) • Alan Feldman

A Sail to Great Island (FP) • Alan Feldman

The Word We Used for It (B) • Max Garland

A Field Guide to the Heavens (B) • Frank X. Gaspar

The Royal Baker's Daughter (FP) • Barbara Goldberg

Gloss • Rebecca Hazelton

Funny (FP) • Jennifer Michael Hecht

The Legend of Light (FP) • Bob Hicok

Sweet Ruin (B) • Tony Hoagland

Partially Excited States (FP) • Charles Hood

Ripe (FP) • Roy Jacobstein

Saving the Young Men of Vienna (B) • David Kirby

Ganbatte (FP) • Sarah Kortemeier

Falling Brick Kills Local Man (FP) • Mark Kraushaar

Last Seen (FP) • Jacqueline Jones LaMon

The Lightning That Strikes the Neighbors' House (FP) • Nick Lantz

You, Beast (B) • Nick Lantz

The Explosive Expert's Wife • Shara Lessley

The Unbeliever (B) • Lisa Lewis

Slow Joy (B) • Stephanie Marlis

Acts of Contortion (B) • Anna George Meek

Bardo (B) • Suzanne Paola

Meditations on Rising and Falling (B) • Philip Pardi

Old and New Testaments (B) • Lynn Powell

Season of the Second Thought (FP) • Lynn Powell

A Path between Houses (B) • Greg Rappleye

The Book of Hulga (FP) • Rita Mae Reese

Why Can't It Be Tenderness (FP) • Michelle Brittan Rosado

Don't Explain (FP) • Betsy Sholl

House of Sparrows: New and Selected Poems (4L) • Betsy Sholl

Late Psalm • Betsy Sholl

Otherwise Unseeable (4L) • Betsy Sholl

Blood Work (FP) • Matthew Siegel

The Year We Studied Women (FP) • Bruce Snider

Bird Skin Coat (B) • Angela Sorby

The Sleeve Waves (FP) • Angela Sorby

If the House (B) • Molly Spencer

Wait (B) • Alison Stine

Hive (B) • Christina Stoddard

The Red Virgin: A Poem of Simone Weil (B) • Stephanie Strickland

The Room Where I Was Born (B) • Brian Teare

Fragments in Us: Recent and Earlier Poems (FP) • Dennis Trudell

The Apollonia Poems (4L) • Judith Vollmer

Level Green (B) • Judith Vollmer

Reactor • Judith Vollmer

Voodoo Inverso (FP) • Mark Wagenaar

Hot Popsicles • Charles Harper Webb

Liver (FP) • Charles Harper Webb

The Blue Hour (B) • Jennifer Whitaker

Centaur (B) • Greg Wrenn

Pocket Sundial (B) • Lisa Zeidner